GRANT

-v-

MAYTAG

YOMI MAKANJUOLA

GRANT-v-MAYTAG

© *Yomi Makanjuola 2018*
First published by Margin Writers in March 2018

All rights reserved, including the right to reproduce this book or portions thereof in any form whatsoever.

Cover design by CreateSpace

Manufactured in the UK by CreateSpace

Order paperback and e-Book versions at www.amazon.com

Delphic Inspiration

From

The Bern Patent Office 'Cobbler'

(circa 1902)

CHAPTER 1

Like teardrops in a rainstorm, Robbie's childhood was engulfed and ruined by his father's overbearing shadow. Other than stolen escape into cyberspace and fantasyland, his existence was plagued with angst. The rancid plume was of such a nature and intensity that, years later, bad memories bubbled to the surface at the most unexpected moments. Six months after his sixteenth birthday, Robbie left home with the intention of never returning.

To help you picture what life was like in their household, Robbie was inclined to describe his father as his personal *Anton Chigurh*, a constant stalker he imagined he would never evade in this life, and maybe not in the next. His father had a weakness for crew cuts, and would never have worn a hideous toupee. Also, he refrained from rawhide boots, and did not own a pneumatic stun gun; nevertheless, he harboured deep sadism and oozed naked aggression. Robbie often pictured his father, shorn of his family, living in a land inhabited by mean and loathsome old men.

Father, okay Pop, as his children called him though not necessarily out of affection, had served in the Royal Navy for about five years. For as long as Robbie could remember, Pop regaled him and his brothers with astounding tales of his maritime experience. Seaman Robert James Grant, Bob to his mates, claimed that he was decommissioned in the process of decades-long downsizing of Britain's once-proud, all-conquering navy. In reality, he was dishonourably discharged for misconduct and lack of professionalism. Only his wife had the faintest idea that Pop was dismissed following a mysterious disagreement with his Petty Officer. Pop never went into details except to hint that he had been pushed to the wall, and had no alternative but to retaliate. Incidentally, his children were not privy to their father's disgrace.

One other fascinating legacy from Pop's navy days were the tattoos on his forearms, a standard indulgence of sailors from time immemorial. However, this period was at least two or three decades before tattoos became part of mainstream Western culture. In their local community, Pop's distinctive blue octopus and orca tattoos were a source of constant bemusement to many.

After spending ten weeks at the maritime training centre at Raleigh, south west England, Pop's active service in the Royal Navy began as part of NATO's deployment to the Baltic Sea. At the height of the *Cold War*, this region represented the so-called trip wire between the Soviet Union and Western Europe. However, after the fall of the Berlin Wall, NATO's patrol exercises reduced significantly which meant that crew members of HMS Lionheart spent more time onshore in countries such as Finland and Sweden. It was during this period that Pop began to explore Scandinavian history and culture, in the shadow of larger and more powerful neighbours like Russia and Germany. Rather than travel back to England for his leave, mostly he preferred to spend days on end roaming the streets of Helsinki, Malmo, and adjoining towns.

Skills-wise, Pop trained as a cook in the navy. Nobody's fool, he leveraged his culinary skills in wooing and later marrying Mary Frost, whom he met in the seaside city of Brighton. Afterwards, the couple chose to settle down in one of the neighbourhoods adjoining the centre of Brighton, renowned as a tourist attraction for millions of foreign and domestic fun-seekers. Pop became a licensed butcher and thus began the legendary career, at least in his own mind, of *Butcher Bob*. Reputed to have as many as 4,000 restaurants, Pop could be deemed to have been strategic in his choice of Brighton as his business location.

Over time, *Butcher Bob* became a moderately successful local brand, selling everything from poultry, fish, lamb, to British beef. In the summer, the store also sold ice cream, not retail but in wholesale gallons. From the start, Pop made a big bet by investing in a walk-in freezer or cold room that was more than twice the volume required for his size of operations. Essentially, he ploughed the bulk of his savings and what he was able to borrow from family and friends into what became the heart of *Butcher Bob*. Subsequently christened *Ingrid*, Pop loved to tell the story of how he acquired the freezer. What his listeners, including his wife and children, did not realise was that Pop held back the most crucial part of his backstory.

The incident that led to Pop's ejection from the Royal Navy centred on his contentious relationship with Petty Officer Sean Angus, a Scot, who managed the ship's galley where all the meals were prepared. To be sure, Sean had no problem with Pop's work ethic. However, he could not stand Pop's brash and patronising attitude, a trait which the latter tried to cover up with his phony sense of humour. Pop seemed able to fool most crew members but Sean was on to him. Cannily, Sean ensured that Pop's workload exceeded the benchmark and refused to cut him any slack whatsoever. On occasions, Pop challenged Sean's order without being openly insubordinate.

The ship's galley had a walk-in freezer where all the food supplies were stored. One Saturday, after the ship had replenished its food supply, Pop and a colleague were designated for stock-taking. This task was rotated among the kitchen staff, although Pop felt that he was being slated more than others. At well below freezing point, those assigned to this job wore special protective gear but, despite this, they rarely spent more than a few minutes deep inside the freezer before exiting, and then returning. After the stock-taking, Sean would show up to conduct a final inspection, before signing off. On this fateful day, Sean was running late for an officers' meeting. After a perfunctory peep into the inner bulk area where huge cartons blocked his view, he bolted the door shut, without realising that Pop was still inside.

Ten minutes later, when Pop's workmate noticed that Pop had not returned to their pad, he took the initiative to search for him. Meanwhile, Pop had tried to manipulate the lock mechanism from the inside without any luck, and had begun to bang on the door. Save for his protective gear and the fortunate intervention of his colleague, Pop believed that he would have frozen to death. Subsequently, a thorough investigation was conducted, leading to an official reprimand of Petty Officer Angus. Close to experiencing frost bite on his hands, and mentally unbalanced, Pop could not shake the suspicion that Sean had deliberately locked him inside the freezer. Of course, he could not prove such a grave allegation, and even though Sean apologised, Pop simply could not let go.

Two weeks later, Pop ambushed Sean in an isolated part of the ship. Muttering under his breath, he attacked Sean with a cricket bat, which he had borrowed from the ship's gymnasium. Blindsided, Sean was bloodied but fought back to save himself from Pop's manic fury. Following another investigation and the submission of a report to the ship's Commanding Officer, a hearing was held before a disciplinary panel that recommended severe sanctions for the perpetrator. After being ratified by the executive committee, Pop's naval career was terminated, effective immediately, without any option for an appeal. The official conclusion was that revenge was his primary motive therefore his navy counsel's application for a psychiatrist evaluation was rejected.

A few years later, as he sought to jump-start his new career, Pop had an interesting frame of reference when talking about his knowledge and passion for industrial freezers,

"Egyptians are to tent-making what the Scandinavians are to freezer design. For centuries, the best decorative and quality tent design originated from Egypt, which should not be a surprise considering the parched weather in the Middle East. Likewise, the Finns and Swedes, in particular, are renowned for the most innovative freezer designs because of their proximity to harsh wintry weather."

Huh? Whenever Pop made such cryptic pronouncements, he probably did so armed with the logic that no one could fact-check him. And it would not have mattered anyway, since his audience hardly ever comprised his intellectual peers.

Anyway, when the time came for Pop to procure an industrial freezer for his new business, he sought out a Finnish company, *Porkka*, that specialised in custom-built products. The design he selected had three compartments. Farthest from the access area was the chilliest storage space, adjacent to the primary and most voluminous compartment. Regulated to operate at -10ºC, the middle chamber was designed to hold animal products. The front area preceding the access door was basically a staging area, where items retrieved from storage could be temporarily kept.

The temperature of the staging area could be controlled to operate at close to ambient when the inner door is sealed up. Constructed with state-of-the-art thermal insulation materials, Pop recognised that the durability of his business venture depended on the quality of his storage freezer. Therefore, he was fully involved in the planning, design and production stages, visiting Finland twice whilst the construction was in progress. At the commissioning, Pop and his new wife invited family, friends, business associates, as well as prospective customers.

So, well before Harry, Robbie and Jack were conceived, the raffish side of Pop had christened his deep freezer *Ingrid*, a traditional Scandinavian name. Ostensibly, the boys had a big, elder sister who, as time passed, they came to dread and even hate with unrestrained passion.

CHAPTER 2

As the second of three boys, Robbie was christened Robert Jay Grant in the Church of England, unlike mononymous *Ingrid*. It was his mother's idea to name him Robert after her grandfather, although people simply assumed that Robbie was Robert, Jnr. At school, and in their neighbourhood, he could remember being called Bert, Bertie, Rob, Bobby, and all the way back to Robert. With his concealed animus towards his father, he hated the fact that they shared the same name. After leaving home, he weighed up the option but his tepid attempt to recast himself as Jay fizzled fast, so Robbie he remained.

Separated on either side from Robbie by two years, it seemed that Harry, Robbie and Jack were born in lockstep to serve Pop's regimented and obsessive compulsive personality. When their mother wondered out loud how Pop would have reacted had they had only girls, Pop retorted, *"Nah! Not this thoroughbred!"* Silly and shallow, this statement made no sense at so many levels, but who was there to challenge him in his own household. Pop was certainly no thoroughbred, whatever he implied by it. Unburdened by any ancestral pedigree of note, Pop was however a proud and highly patriotic Englishman. In his own mind, he believed that his Englishness placed him at the apex of the human food chain, despite his poor education, grating ignorance, and lack of introspection.

With his military background, it was no surprise that Pop turned out to be a ramrod enforcer, whose parental skills and code of discipline borrowed liberally from a navy warrant officer's manual. After kindergarten, the boys were introduced to what Pop termed the drill. For *The Sound of Music* aficionados, the movie reflects what the Grant family drill was like. That being the case, Pop lacked *Baron von Trapp*'s class or his Teutonic mien. Nevertheless, Pop's provincial mantra was resonant: *"there's no room in this house for sissies."* By the time Robbie turned six, Pop introduced him and Harry to drill commands, issued randomly - before meals, before bedtime, *after* watching a movie, or frankly anytime Pop was in the mood to indulge his eccentricity.

If Robbie lived to be a hundred, he was certain he could never escape the barking orders: *"Fall in," "Attention," "March," "Mark time," "Stand easy,"* and so on, ringing in his ears. Hard to imagine perhaps but come rain, sunshine or snow, Robbie grew up to associate their back garden not with flowers, but with misery and torment. Indeed, his impulse to flee took root in that garden.

In contrast, Harry's staccato chuckles during drill sessions conveyed the impression that he was having the time of his life. Or was he? If Robbie struggled to retain his sanity, was Harry's chuckling a sign that his mind was slowly dissolving despite the brave front? Unable to deter Pop, their mother attempted to shield her youngest child, Jack, for as long as possible. However, three months after Jack reached the magic age of six, all bets were off. From Pop's perspective, only the strong and gutsy deserve to survive in this world, and he wanted to ensure that his children turned out hard as nails.

Frequently subjected to Pop's rhetorical flourish, the boys were captive to their father's predilection for World War II stories, which he described as a real war in contrast with the subsequent *Cold War* stalemate between the U.S. and the Soviet Union. A recycled anecdote that he believed would help his sons develop good survival instincts went as follows:

"The world out there is twisted and unforgiving... you've got to be smart. Never allow anyone, especially those in positions of authority, to push you around if you can help it. Remember, the first wave of soldiers at the Normandy landing was cut down. The second wave stood a fighting chance. Better still, be part of the fourth wave..."

Pop was one of those parents who rarely provided context when talking to their children. He enjoyed the sound of his voice far too much, and did everyone not know about Normandy? In his opinion, kids are like sponges capable of absorbing much of what is thrown at them, and then grow up to re-use whatever they found useful. Besides, his sons were very fortunate indeed because his own father was usually too drunk to spend quality time with him and his six siblings.

The earlier reference to *Anton Chigurh* was not meant to be flippant. As far as Robbie could tell, Pop and Mary had radically different views about parenting, and often argued about one lunatic idea or the other. Channelling his inner *Chigurh*, Pop was a ludicrous mimic with an anti-artistry manner all of his own. Often, he would end family debates by calling out, *"Heads or tails?"* and with little originality pull out a coin. Through it all, one specific incident became etched into Robbie's subconscious. While their mother was out one day, after drill practice, Pop lined up his three boys and pronounced,

"Harry, you I get... you are the head. Jack, I also understand... you represent the tail. But what does that make you, Robbie? I never could figure you out."

Surely, one had to wonder what type of father would refer to his own child as the *tail*, and another as a nonentity. Someone who is psychologically damaged? Deeply hurt, Pop's mad taunt left an emotional scar on Robbie which thankfully lost its sting as time passed. He could never comprehend why Pop seemed to pick on him more than his siblings. While he had a decent relationship with Jack, Harry was another story entirely. To his credit, Harry appeared to have developed a higher threshold for pain than his younger brothers. Always eager to please Pop, the glint in Harry's eyes and his flinty expression perplexed Robbie, who could not mask his own distress.

While the sibling rivalry between Harry and Robbie was persistent, the frequency of their scuffles subsided when, by his fourteenth birthday, Robbie had grown taller and bigger than his elder brother. After losing his physical edge, Harry resorted to mental intimidation, straight out of Pop's playbook. Well aware of Harry's lack of imagination and creativity, Robbie found his *James Cagney* imitation poses more laughable than menacing.

The Grants lived in a residential neighbourhood that abutted a commercial district while the boys attended Patcham High School, which was less than half a kilometre from their father's shop. *Butcher Bob*, in turn, was located along bustling London Road close to the Brighton Rail Station. Though nominally a housewife, Mary threw herself into the family business, as did all of them. Rising as early as 5:00 a.m. in the early days, Robbie's parents worked very long hours at the store. As the business expanded, two workers were formally employed. One covered the morning shift usually fronted by Pop, while the other supported Mary who ran the store from around 2:00 p.m. until 6:00 p.m., Monday through Friday. The shift hands tidied up and closed up the store around 8:00 p.m. During school term, each of the boys put in a one hour shift, twice a week, while not forgetting that they still needed to do their homework.

Saturday was their parents' rest day, though the store's busiest, when the workers mostly ran *Butcher Bob*. Although Mary hardly ever showed up at the store on weekends, Pop would typically pop in and out, with one or three of his boys in tow. Naturally, the boys would have preferred to be out playing or watching football with their friends, but Pop preached the creed of enterprise before pleasure. Pertaining to pleasure, it is often said that familiarity can breed contempt. Having grown up within spitting distance of the West Pier, the Brighton Palace Pier, and other famous tourist sites, the appeal had long worn off.

Back at the store, Sundays were eerily silent but Saturdays held great dread for the boys at *Butcher Bob's* because of what became known as the *Ingrid treatment*.

Professional psychologists will probably have a field day analysing Pop's psyche, and a researcher could write a dissertation in the process. On the other hand, pop psychologists, with no reputation to protect, might simply classify Pop's disciplinary actions as child abuse. With scant warning, any of the boys could be called to account for some misdeed or the other committed during the outgoing week. As punishment, the culprit was banished to the *Ingrid* staging compartment for upwards of fifteen minutes under moderately cool conditions.

Granted that Pop was not crazy enough to risk any of his sons' lives but could it be that, perversely, he was re-enacting and reliving the trauma he experienced in the belly of HMS Lionheart through his children?

Had this bizarre 'punishment' been reported to Children's Social Services, Pop would most definitely have been hung up to freeze like the beef carcasses inside *Ingrid*. Strangely, none of the boys ever disclosed Pop's handiwork to their mother, while the store workers simply minded their own business. In any case, what finally and mercifully put paid to the *Ingrid treatment* happened a few months before Robbie turned sixteen. For the first and last time, Pop simultaneously locked up Harry and Robbie inside *Ingrid*, in what turned out to be a very bad idea, considering the simmering tension between the brothers.

Cooped up and with nowhere to go, Harry could not resist needling Robbie. When Robbie finally snapped, the ensuing fistfight continued until Pop, hearing the commotion, unlocked the entrance door. Bloodied but unbowed, each had given as good as he received. The tussle was almost reminiscent of Joe Frazier's refusal to bend to Muhammad Ali's will at the end of the *Thrilla in Manilla*. By the time Pop popped open the access door, Robbie had made up his mind to leave home as soon as feasible. In short, he had reached his limit with his father, Harry, and *Ingrid*. That was all there was to it.

CHAPTER 3

Mary Grant was apoplectic when she discovered what had happened to her eldest sons at *Butcher Bob*. Not only was it left to her to patch up Harry and Robbie, without drawing undue attention from neighbours, but she also had to concoct the old influenza excuse as to why they missed school for three straight days the following week.

Their mother was so upset that she did not speak to Pop for close to two weeks. Ultimately, she managed to win a long-sought concession from him that stopped the boys from working at the store on Saturdays. Though Pop appeared chastened by the incident, but secretly he was delighted. Essentially, he viewed it a sign of the boys' growing ability to stand up for themselves, and nothing more than a coming-of-age brawl. Though Harry's gruff attitude remained intact, his admiration for his brother grew ever so grudgingly.

In the aftermath, the most articulate of the whole bunch, Jack, came up with the phrase *Frigid Ingrid*, which initially went straight over Robbie's head. In his inestimable mind, Jack surmised that

Ingrid, with a personality all of her own, had remained unresponsive and aloof throughout the fight. By not lifting a finger, *Frigid Ingrid* therefore became a willing accessory to Pop's assault on his own children. As for Robbie, the event merely motivated him to start plotting his escape from a toxic environment. Besides, he had no intention of working in, or ever taking over, his father's business.

Ironically, Pop's malevolence indirectly contributed to Robbie's career plans. At school, few if any of their mates would wilfully challenge the Grant boys. Aside from Harry who could be menacing even without being provoked, Robbie and Jack were tough nuts who held their ground in any physical confrontation. If Pop deserved some credit for breeding stand-up fighters, another facet of home life where Pop's influence was tolerant and indelible was film consumption. Though the family rarely patronised movie theatres, what passed for quality time with the children was Pop bringing home rented DVDs, supplemented with feature films on television. By the time they were out of nappies, the boys grew up on a steady diet of cartoons and action movies. When smart phones and broadband services became ubiquitous, Robbie discovered that Pop's marginal interest in technology allowed him unfettered access to online content. Apart from action movies, Robbie also enjoyed comedies and other genres like adventure and science fiction.

Time spent with Pop eating popcorn and swapping movie titbits was the most free-wheeling in their household, and embodied Robbie's most cherished memories. Conversely, school was always a hard slug due to Robbie's dyslexia. Though diagnosed as mildly severe, he was fortunate that he grew up when dyslexia had become part of school lexicon. Twenty years earlier, and before then, he might have been labelled as stupid. With the help of therapists, Robbie's reading ability improved but his interest in intellectual pursuits was greatly curtailed.

As far back as he could recall, Robbie hankered to become a film actor. Modesty aside, he thought he had the looks, the acting ability and, later, the physique to give it a shot. However, by age thirteen, his interest shifted decidedly towards becoming a stuntman. He discovered that the movie stars and entertainers that charmed him the most were actors like Jackie Chan, Hal Needham, the late Dar Robinson, and not forgetting the legendary Evel Knievel. Pop and all the Grant boys were huge fans of Knievel, but Robbie became highly infatuated as a kid when he learnt that 'Evel' was in fact the motorcycle stunt wizard Robert Craig Knievel's adopted name.

At first, the path to a career as a stuntman was a mystery to Robbie. But he was smart enough to figure out that he needed to achieve at least basic GCSE qualifications, if he planned to attend a formal acting school. At school, he enjoyed the History and English Literature classes. But by a stretch, he was passionate about the drama programme offered by his school. A favourite of virtually all his drama teachers, Robbie brought a focus and intensity to his performance that impressed his instructors. One or two of them would have been baffled if they discovered that Robbie was not angling to become his generation's Laurence Olivier but rather wished to emulate Vic Armstrong, credited as the most prolific stuntman by the Guinness Book of Records.

Since none of the school plays he participated in contained roles written for stuntmen, Robbie had no choice but to portray mainstream characters. His most high-profile role was Mark Anthony in the school's adaptation of *Julius Caesar*. Over a period of four months of rehearsals,

Robbie was exempted from afternoon duty at *Butcher Bob*. Pop was not particularly enthused when Robbie brought home an official letter from school, informing his parents about the extracurricular demand on his time.

Unlike Pop, Mary prompted and encouraged Robbie throughout this period and was genuinely proud of his achievement. At the play's opening, she sat in the section reserved for parents while Jack was also there to lend his support. Whether intentional or not, Pop and Harry chose that Saturday evening to be at *Butcher Bob* to supervise the servicing of *Ingrid*. The process was scheduled to end by 5:00 p.m. but the technicians overran by over two hours. Their absence, and coincidence, was not lost on Robbie, and it only reinforced his alienation from both his father and older brother.

On the sports front, Pop tried to steer his boys towards rugby, which he touted as quintessential English. As they grew older, Harry embraced rugby and developed into a recognised jock in the local school community. On his part, Robbie preferred football and trampolining, a fringe sport that caught his attention due to the gym teacher's infectious enthusiasm. Able to connect the dots, Robbie reasoned that trampolining would teach him the art of jumping and falling whilst avoiding injury – a useful skill for a budding stuntman.

Mr. Maurice Pitt had tried out for the Olympics but just failed to make the grade. From him, Robbie picked up the basic techniques and conditioning needed to execute simple jumps in straight, tuck, pike, and straddle positions. To ensure participants' health and safety, the school discouraged complex somersaults. Since the operative word was complex, it was impossible to stop the kids from performing high twists, and the occasional somersaults, without the knowledge of their instructors.

When Robbie's mother asked him what he wanted for his fourteenth birthday, he did not hesitate, *"Please, mum, can you get me a trampoline?"* He had been nursing the idea of a trampoline in their back garden so that he could practise at home. Replied Mary, *"A trampoline? Well, you know I'd have to ask your father."* Pop's response was not a surprise,

"What on earth do you want a blooming trampoline for? First, it will take up the whole of our garden... secondly, it reminds me of

synchronised swimming... way too girlish, if you ask me."

This was at dinner and Robbie knew better than to argue with his father, who rarely ever lost an argument, especially when money was a defining factor. In a flash, Robbie invoked Plan B, *"In that case, Pop, can I have a BMX bike?"* Since Jack had received one for his last birthday, Pop did not object, and that was that.

Inadvertently Pop had unleashed the *Evel* in his two younger sons. Weather permitting, most afternoons after school - before or after taking turns at the store - Robbie and Jack engaged in their own versions of daredevil stunts, ranging from the classic *bunny hop*, the oddly-named *nollie*, which is the opposite of the *bunny hop*, to the *fakie*. All these tricks involved somehow getting the bike wheels off the ground, but the *fakie* took the crown because it demanded pushing off a wall and riding backwards to gain momentum. Harry never liked bikes, a fact that suited Robbie perfectly. In later years, he would recall the time he spent with Jack ramping up their bikes as part of the happiest of his childhood.

On Robbie's fourteenth birthday, which fell on a Sunday, Pop was in an unusually good mood.

Their mother had made the usual roast beef and ordered a birthday cake. Even Harry displayed what passed for his best behaviour. As subdued as he was ever likely to be, he still could not help interjecting the odd snide remark. After desserts, just before they settled down to watch a movie, Pop shared an anecdote which Robbie thought contained probably the most important lesson he ever learnt from his father.

His family had known for some time that one of Pop's all-time favourite actors was Michael Caine. To him, Caine's irrepressible cockney accent set him apart from those he liked to describe as phony Hollywood transplants. In any case, Caine had distinguished himself in films such as Get Carter, Italian Job, Educating Rita, Alfie, and a range of other great movies, all of which the Grant boys had watched with their father. During this teachable moment, thankfully Pop did not evoke his rather awful imitation of Caine's inflection,

"Michael Caine was once on a film set with this great director, whose reputation was such that virtually everyone felt intimidated in his presence. Incidentally, I've forgotten her name... in any case, Caine's co-star was a nervous wreck before each take. In one scene, this female star was expected to

walk through a door into a room where Caine was seated. Anyway, there was this chair prop close to the entrance. Every time the lead actress entered the room, she would knock over this chair and then stop. As jumpy as a kitten, this charade occurred three times, before Caine stepped in to calm her down.

Apparently, Michael Caine said to the lady, 'Why don't you use the difficulty?' She responded, 'Huh?' Caine reiterated, 'I was once told that if I ever got into trouble, I should simply use the difficulty. An obstacle does not have to become an immovable barrier. Now, if the chair should fall over again, just assume that was the intention all along and carry on.' Well, believe it or not, it worked, and the director played right along.

The point of the story is that, in life, things do not always turn out as planned. In such situations, I want you to learn how to 'use the difficulty' and get on with it. Never moan... like most people do, claiming that life isn't fair. Of course, life isn't fair!"

Robbie loved the story, despite his antipathy towards his father. Meanwhile, to Pop, the story demonstrated how unpretentious, as he put it,

Michael Caine was. Possibly, Pop saw Caine reflected in his own no-nonsense attitude to life. Even after Michael Caine began to appear in movies such as *Inception*, *Interstellar* and the *Batman* series, all standard Hollywood fare, Pop kept faith with his ultimate cockney hero.

Come to think of it, Robbie could pass for a young Michael Caine - without the glasses -which was not the worst compliment for an aspiring actor.

CHAPTER 4

Michael Caine look-alike or not, Robbie was intelligent enough to realise that it would take more than sharp looks to succeed in life. Like Caine, he had an air of confidence and easy charm about him, and whether he admitted it or not, Robbie was also very ambitious. He was determined to break into the film industry, starting in England and eventually winding his way to Hollywood, fingers crossed. True, he longed to make it as a stuntman but, deep down, he also wanted to be taken seriously as a professional actor.

Knowing that he was an above average student, if he pushed himself, Robbie however had no strong desire to attend university. In contrast, Jack was a veritable high-flyer who was always near the top of his class. Leaning more towards arts rather than science subjects, Robbie did just enough to pass his GCSE with six credits. Instead of proceeding to the two-year advanced level programme, his plan was to take a year off before attending a vocational college that offered basic training in drama and creative arts. Considering his parents' background, there was no undue pressure for either Harry or Robbie to pursue an academic career. While Harry seemed content to stay close to the family business, Jack was so brilliant that their parents expected him to be the first member of their extended family to attend university. In truth, no one paid much heed to Robbie's career prospects, which in a way suited him just fine.

When Robbie began plotting his escape in earnest, the greatest challenge he faced was undoubtedly financial. Also, until he turned eighteen, he could not apply for social housing. Compounding his next move was his desire to keep a fair distance between himself and his father, since he could not predict how Pop might react. What boosted Robbie's confidence as he contemplated the unknown was the fact that he knew someone who had blazed the same path ahead of him. To be more specific, Zac Levin, a former schoolmate and friend who was three years older than Robbie, had remained on his radar screen. If in fact opposites attract, Robbie and Zac possessed contrasting attributes, at least in terms of physical appearance. While Robbie was a shade above six feet tall, with some room to grow, Zac was a compact five-foot six with distinctive curly hair, who was blessed with abundant street smarts.

Zac never knew his father. He was the first child of a single mother who ended up with two other children, a boy and a girl, for two other men. Home was never a bed of roses and, without a father figure around, he grew up fast on the streets. Money was always tight, although his mother did her utmost as a provider by sometimes juggling two jobs. To fill the gap, Zac started hustling as early as age thirteen, by buying and selling what he termed hot stuff, not stolen but in high demand. Essentially, he dabbled in products that were popular with teenagers, and built up quite a reputation at his school. Such products ranged from T-shirts, baseball caps, down to lipsticks for the girls.

Smart kid that he was, he avoided the wrath of school authorities by facilitating product-cash exchanges outside the school premises. His promotional appeal emulated the American retailing behemoth, *Walmart*, since his customers knew that Zac offered the best value for money. By selling at extremely low margins, he was able to move large volumes.

Perhaps because of his unconventional upbringing, Zac's moral compass was not exactly pointing due north. From time to time, Zac was known, for example, to sell products that had exceeded their sell-by dates. Personally, he did not deem himself as dishonest because he understood that in the world of commerce, sometimes success or failure required walking a fine line. He also recognised that people could be capricious, often wanting to eat their cake and all that.

Mature beyond his years, Zac had very little affinity for formal education and, as such, left school with only two GCSE pass grades, one of which was in Mathematics. Blessed with a head for numbers, Zac's business instincts were like quicksilver which was why more academically gifted classmates voted him as one of the most likely to succeed in their cohort.

Like most students at Patcham High School, it was virtually impossible not to know Zac. By virtue of his *Butcher Bob* exposure, Robbie was genuinely fascinated by Zac's business acumen, which no other student came close to demonstrating, at least that early. Although his future interests lay elsewhere, Robbie was intrigued by Zac who, in turn, admired his younger friend's acting ability and passion for the film industry.

When Zac vacated his mother's council flat, he moved into a house in Hove, where rents were relatively affordable. As the boundaries of Brighton had expanded, the authorities decided by the turn of the last century to create a new city called Brighton and Hove, which is quite a mouthful. Anyway, Zac ended up in a rather large building rented out to mostly young people, a few of whom were petty traders like Zac. Zac occupied a two-bedroom flat, using the smaller one as his stockroom. From his savings, he was able to buy a second-hand Nissan station wagon that provided much-needed mobility for business and pleasure.

On the day Robbie moved out, he planned it such that Zac arrived at their front door soon after his mother departed for her afternoon shift at *Butcher Bob*. Robbie had one large suitcase and a general-purpose duffel bag which held most of his non-cloth items. Fortunately, Harry was also at the store at the time and, although Jack was aware of Robbie's ploy, Robbie implored him to leave home with their mother to establish plausible deniability if his parents ever queried him.

More emotional than he thought he would be, Robbie felt a slight pang of regret leaving behind all that he had ever known. However, like Zac, he possessed steely ambition which was a trait they both shared. In terms of their outlook, they were also not far apart, as each seemed to have an ingrained ability to bounce back from life's reversals. As Zac drove, they chatted, or rather Zac hit Robbie with a slew of business ideas and 'hot' prospects, and about how he needed to inject more capital '*to rise to the next level.*' His friend could tell that Zac's appetite for wheeling and dealing had not diminished an iota.

Zac offered to share his two-room apartment with Robbie, rent-free, until he could secure a job and share the burden. Undeterred by manual work, thanks to his *Butcher Bob* experience, Robbie was soon hired by a local supermarket to stack shelves in its warehouse. Although this job paid minimum wage, Robbie had no difficulty adapting to the unusual working hours and earning overtime pay. It was perhaps this can-do attitude that most impressed Zac about Robbie.

As Robbie soon discovered, Zac seemed obsessed by two subjects: Alan Sugar and China. However, before Zac opened the floodgates and literally swamped Robbie with his schemes, he shared a personal detail that, at first, did not resonate with his friend. One Sunday afternoon, while relaxing in their flat, Zac suddenly blurted out,

"Did I ever tell you that I am a Jew?"

"No, not really… Er, but why are you telling me now?"

"I am not that religious. In fact, I am not religious at all and I have never really explored my Jewishness, except that my mother told me that my father, who I have never met, was… is a Jew. Of course, I'm very conscious of the historical fact that Jews were always a minority group in Europe but it's not been a factor in my life, one way or another. Can't really explain why, but can you believe that you are the first person I am sharing this with?" continued Zac.

"OK, I hear you… neither is my family that religious, except that I know that I was baptised… but my last church attendance was my grandmother's funeral a couple of years ago. But you still have not told me what brought this on."

"Have you heard of a British businessman called Alan Sugar? He anchors the reality TV show, The Apprentice?"

Robbie was aware of the TV series but unfamiliar with the cast. He nodded unenthusiastically and, with scant interruption, Zac's monologue took off,

"Well, let me tell you about him... OK, I have taken the time to find out as much as I could about him, and I am not embarrassed to describe him as my role model.

I discovered that, like me, Alan Sugar also comes from a Jewish family and that he quit school at 16, which seems to be a rite of passage of sorts for enterprising young people.

Long before he became a business icon and billionaire, Alan Michael Sugar started out as a scrappy seller of low-cost consumer electronic products like amplifiers, tuners, and stereo equipment, all sourced from the Far East. Branding his products Amstrad, a play on his initials, later he launched a personal computer model during the early phase of the PC revolution.

You know what, no one ever accused Alan Sugar of being a technology innovator. His insight was to spot market opportunities, secure suppliers at source, and badge affordable products of decent quality to compete with the market leaders."

At that point, Robbie interrupted his friend with the question,

"So, how did he transform from all that to become a TV reality show personality?"

"The way I understand it, after his business success, Mr. Sugar could not escape the attention of politicians. No, he did not formally go into politics but has been known to support through donations causes that he cares about. Anyhow, when the search was on for someone to chair the boardroom of the UK version of The Apprentice, modelled after the part played by Donald Trump in the US, Alan Sugar's name was on the shortlist. After he was drafted, and starting in 2005, he has fronted the show. Not only does the winner receive a cash prize but also an opportunity to work in one of Mr. Sugar's subsidiary companies as an 'apprentice'. Well, you could say that the show provides Mr. Sugar with a platform for encouraging young entrepreneurs, and an opportunity to polish his own personal brand."

"I get it," responded Robbie, smiling, *"and I suppose you are the next Alan Sugar, is that it?"*

"You can laugh all you want, but what really caught my attention about his business career was

how he exploited opportunities in Taiwan and the Far East, well before China became what is now called 'The World's Workshop.'

I'm sure that you are aware that the Industrial Revolution began here in Britain in the 18th century, the site of the original workshop, so to speak. Anyway, in the past twenty to thirty years, China has become the go-to place for aspiring entrepreneurs based on the sheer size and dynamism of its market. The reason I am excited about China is because what Alan Sugar imagined thirty years ago is even more relevant today. Today, China is the second largest economy in the world, having overtaken Britain, Germany and Japan within a generation. Amazing!"

"*Have you been to China, by any chance?*" asked Robbie.

"*Twice actually and, one of these days, I'd like you to come along, if you'd like to join me.*

Let's chill out for a bit... Later this evening, I will tell you all about Guangzhou, one of the most incredible places on this planet, believe me."

After dinner, Zac picked up where he left off,

"Guangzhou, I guess it takes some practice to learn how to pronounce Chinese words... Are you aware that Mandarin is the official language in China, spoken by over 1 billion people, which is quite mind-boggling. As I was saying, Guangzhou is recognised as the manufacturing hub of the world... it is a mind-boggling city in the southern province of Guangdong. Guangdong, itself, has a population of over 100 million people, which is larger than Germany, the biggest EU country. Another reason why Guangdong is so hot is its proximity to another fast-growing city, Shenzhen, which is just across the border from Hong Kong.

Without exaggeration, almost anything and everything is manufactured and exported from Guangdong, aided by its access to the South China Sea coastline. Having visited Guangdong twice, I can tell you that it has the feel and all the buzz of any big Western city – cool skyline, great transportation, international restaurants, and affordable hotels. But, more than all that, Chinese manufacturers are unbeatable when it comes to manufacturing on demand, and shipping via the Internet.

Traders with original, or sometimes stolen, product designs can find willing Chinese partners who are not bothered about intellectual property rights. Without owning a factory, warehouse, or a supply chain, enterprising entrepreneurs can build websites through which they can fulfil orders received from customers. It is truly mind-blowing.

Now, with e-Commerce and platforms like Alibaba.com now available, thousands of businesspeople from all over the world now flock to Guangdong and its trade shows. The scenario is completely different from what a young Alan Sugar would have encountered back in the 1980s, that's for sure."

As Zac paused to catch his breath, Robbie noticed that two of Zac's favourite words were 'mind-blowing' and 'mind-boggling'. Like a chirpy chappie, he also liked to say, "*He who dares, wins!*" Despite himself, he found Zac's knowledge and enthusiasm quite infectious. Just to needle him a bit, Robbie asked him,

"*So, when do you plan to make your first million pounds, then?*"

"*Jokes apart, it's a great question. The simple barrier is 'capital'. I have loads of great product ideas that I would like to introduce into the UK market. But, in order to set establish and prime my supply chain, I require more capital than I currently have.*

You can imagine that it's not as if I can walk up to my bank manager and ask for a loan. Even if I write a great business plan, getting a bank or investors interested is a tall order. But, I tell you, grabbing the opportunities that I see, that I can almost taste, is all I dream about. Now, I suppose you have a pretty good idea what drives and motivates me. I hope I haven't been a bore.

I imagine that my passion for business is equivalent to your desire to become an actor, or should I say a stuntman, something that is way beyond the realm of my imagination."

"I agree... with your focus and your determination, and remembering what you were like in school, I honestly don't see how anything can stop you. Sure, I'd love to travel to China with you one of these days. It should be quite an adventure. In the meantime, I need to hit the sack since I have to get up early tomorrow."

"Gee, you are right... the weekend is all gone. Good night, buddy."

CHAPTER 5

It is fallacious to suggest that human beings are either good or bad. The duality of saintliness and extreme evil are notional boundaries that shift from one culture to another. In the event, it is virtually impossible to predict how any individual will behave under an infinite set of circumstances. But since no human being is an island and because no two people are wired exactly the same, societies have evolved rules and conventions that attempt to moderate and govern human interaction. Without such statutes, civilisation as we know it could hardly exist.

In many parts of the world, concepts such as democracy, human rights, freedom of the press, and the rule of law might very well be taken for granted. To quote the former British Prime Minister, Wilson Churchill, *"Democracy is the worst form of government, except for all the others."* Indeed, for those people who still live under dictatorships, communism, and oppressive rule, the idea that everyone should be equal under the law is a forlorn principle. Sadly, although most nations declare their fealty to the basic rule of law, often grandly enshrined in their Constitution, very few genuinely promote these universal norms and behaviours.

While no democratic system of government is remotely perfect, it is however generally agreed that nations that support human rights, freedom of expression, and uphold a strong judiciary tend to be more just, stable, open and prosperous. Despite the backdrop of its imperialist and class-ridden past, it could be argued that modern Britain has become a symbol of a relatively fair and decent society. Many of the pillars of the British society were established or reformed following World War II. And although the wealthy and well-connected still have certain privileges, institutions such as the National Health Service, the welfare system, the education system, the civil service, and the judiciary are now geared towards meeting the needs of the average citizen.

Justifiably, the British are very proud of their judicial system, which is held up as one of the most effective in the world. While its citizens may not necessarily be more law-abiding than their compatriots who live under institutions tainted by corruption, the notion that no one is above the law seems ingrained in the British psyche. Like any other bureaucratic system, the British judiciary may sometimes seem hidebound, but anyone who dares to skirt around the law or play close to the edge of probity can expect the long arm of law to catch up with them, sooner or later.

From the perspective of most ordinary citizens, including youngsters like Robbie and Zac, law and order was a part of the fabric of the society that was taken for granted. Different from countries with murky undersides, where policemen carry firearms and are highly visible, the image of the British constable, or 'bobby', is a truncheon-carrying public figure on the beat. Nevertheless, the criminal justice system, which is underpinned by undercover detectives in support of the magistrate and high courts, is as busy as anywhere else in the world. Similarly, the civil courts exist to ensure that citizens' human and civil rights are upheld. Older and more experienced than Robbie, Zac had far more exposure to the commercial world, government regulations, and their interfaces with the justice system. For a budding entrepreneur, such awareness would prove invaluable in the long run.

For Robbie, his focus was narrower and more mundane. Although news occasionally reached him about the family he left behind through Jack, he was intent on looking to the future. While he had spoken twice to his mother, he repulsed her overtures to visit him. Truth be told, his main preoccupation was finding the money to pay for his training and development.

After extensive research, he decided on two institutions that offered the requisite technical training to transform him into a professional. The *E15 Acting School* in Loughton was his first choice for two main reasons. Launched over fifty years ago, *E15* is famous for promoting the so-called 'system' or 'method' acting technique invented by the American Mr. Stanislavski. Adopted by many famous stars, such as Marlon Brando, Robert de Niro and Daniel Day-Lewis, the programme is centred on both stage and screen acting. But what sealed it for Robbie was the inclusion of fencing, combat and other action modules in the *E15* curriculum. With perfect timing, Robbie would be eligible to attend *E15* as soon as he turned seventeen, conditional upon him gaining admission and being able to afford the tuition fees.

The second course that he planned to attend was being offered by the foremost stunt training school in the UK, *British Live Action Stunt Training*, otherwise known by the acronym *BLAST*. Aimed at individuals seeking to become professional stunt performers, *BLAST* provides theoretical and practical training taught by film industry experts. Building on a foundation of the highest health and safety standards, trainees are exposed to realistic stunt scenarios designed to test the limits of their mental and physical capabilities. Altogether, Robbie estimated that he would require close to ten thousand pounds for both training courses.

As the weeks went by, Robbie shared his vision and details of his medium-term plans with Zac, who was suitably impressed with his friend's focus and resolve. When Zac asked how Robbie intended to finance his training, and whether he would consider approaching his father for help, Robbie actually laughed out loud before responding,

"No, I'm done with my father... This is all on me. If I start saving now, before too long..."

"Ah, that was precisely what I told myself... about saving up for my proposed ventures in China... I tell you, it's not easy at all. At this rate, after covering our rent and other living expenses, it might take us for ever... and you know that time does not stand still for anyone," interjected Zac.

From that moment onwards, Zac and Robbie started brainstorming and bouncing around plausible ideas that could generate immediate capital to fund their respective projects. While it seemed as if Zac had a better head start to boost his earnings, in fact, he had very low leverage because he had always operated from a small capital base.

While neither Zac nor Robbie would readily admit that he was influenced by the critically acclaimed television series, *Breaking Bad*, it will always remain an open question. The mind, or perhaps the human sub-conscious, is extremely complex and people who do not have strong convictions can easily fall prey to moral relativism. As the world turns or as circumstances change, supposedly fixed principles can become highly subjective.

The main protagonist in *Breaking Bad* was a simple but principled family man, whose promising career trajectory cratered. At fifty years old, he was merely a high school chemistry teacher who was suddenly diagnosed with cancer. The script was considered ground-breaking in exploring a fundamental human dilemma: how elastic are our moral values when we are faced with stark life choices? The pathway from a suburban dad to a cold-hearted drug czar was utterly unpredictable, and could easily have descended into farce on-screen. However, in the hands of a clever and unconventional writer, as well as an exceptional cast, *Breaking Bad* became an instant classic.

Beyond his decision to *break bad* for his family's sake, while his health was deteriorating, Walter White was initially contemptuous of the poor technical skills exhibited by the drug underworld. At some level, Walter felt compelled to show the science illiterates and philistines around him how to produce industrial-grade amphetamines or 'crystal meth'. It could be argued that, at first, the financial benefit was a secondary consideration. Zac and Robbie binge-watched the entire six-part series from Friday evening through Sunday evening, thanks to *Netflix*.

With the passage of time, a sense of urgency crept into their conversations, as the two friends contemplated their next move. Possibly, the same youthful impulse that prompted them to drop out of school made them susceptible to some rather unorthodox ideas. To lighten the mood, Zac suggested that they create five pools into which they could mentally deposit their suggestions: bizarre, reckless, bold, lame, and dumb. Furthermore, to demonstrate how much of the business literature he had assimilated, Zac threw around phrases such as 'risky but high reward', 'pros and cons', 'no percentage in that', and so on.

Over the course of four to five weeks, they eliminated the most extreme of the lot and were soon down to two. Unlike Pop, Robbie did not draw out a coin in the last phase of the decision-making process. Even if the thought crossed his mind, he was way too nervous. Deep down, he knew Zac had already made up his own mind, and he happened to be leaning the same way. It was crunch time.

Two things worried Robbie about their final choice. First, its success or failure rested largely on his shoulders. Second, Zac correctly pointed out that the plan would require a third person, a female accomplice, to provide an air of plausibility. In fact, Zac already had a candidate in mind – a close friend whom he claimed he could trust. They bounced around various scenarios and soon a detailed plan began to emerge. It was time to weaponise their idea. Like Walter White, Robbie's doubts began to dissipate when his perspective shifted to the technical aspects of the challenge before him. He did not feel that Zac had manipulated or brainwashed him at all; rather, the rebellious streak that Pop had inadvertently nurtured convinced him that he could beat the system.

Robbie and Zac had arrived at the first critical crossroads of their short lives, a juncture reeking with moral ambiguity. Daring but not utterly foolish, they were ready to place their bets, while hoping that their cards would come up trumps.

CHAPTER 6

Even for Zac, it would have been a long stretch to imply that *Maytag* was a competitor or a direct threat to his own fledgling business. However, not for nothing had he cultivated a scintilla of the ferocious ambition of another hero of his, Jeff Bezos, the founder and Chairman of *Amazon.com*, the US global retailing giant. The growing dominance of *Amazon* gives the impression of a company that believes that retailing is a zero-sum equation, whereby any dollar that the company fails to attract goes directly to a rival.

In any case, Zac became very conscious of *Maytag* for a simple reason. *Maytag* was a subsidiary of another huge US retailer that was trading under the name *Maytag* in the UK, and had opened its doors to the public less than a year earlier. Branded as a big discounter, the store differentiated itself by locating within Hove, away from the central shopping area in Brighton. Its target market encompassed the working class through to the middle class, young and old. Since its opening, Zac had visited a couple of times and discovered at first-hand how competitive their prices were. This gave him the added impetus to manufacture his own product lines in China, to assure his long-term survival.

The concept of limited liability companies 'trading as' one or multiple other companies is not unique to the UK. Usually, it enables large companies to rebrand and reposition in new markets that may have unique characteristics. Even to those who could be instinctively anti-foreigner or anti-American, *Maytag* was recognised as a modern and hip retail outlet. As much as rivals sought to copy or out-innovate *Maytag*, the fact was that its novelty was yet to wear off.

Ultimately, Zac had a two-part reason for targeting *Maytag*, in the pursuit of their goals. First, *Maytag*'s parent company was highly successful and would be expected to have very deep pockets. Second, the retailer was still relatively new in the UK, and would therefore seek to protect its nascent brand. In other words, a company that had just placed a huge strategic bet, and that was yet to stabilise, was less likely to play hard ball than other players.

Robbie's first encounter with Natalie Jones was brief but startling. She had ridden a bicycle over to their apartment one Saturday evening. According to Zac, she was once his girlfriend but, following an amicable break-up, they had remained good friends not least because their business interests still overlapped. Of average height, Natalie could have been considered beautiful but for her beady mouth and raised eyebrows, which gave her an intense and hardboiled look. Somewhat taciturn, Robbie could detect a lilting accent, later confirmed as Welsh. Natalie was about four months younger than Zac, and just as committed to owning a successful business. Her area of interest was in health food products. Claiming that she had a pending appointment, Natalie spent less than ten minutes before she rode off.

Exactly a week later, Natalie was back in their flat, still hard to read. In the intervening period, Zac had met and discussed the outline of their plan with her. Apparently, she opted in just as Zac had anticipated and, if she had any qualms, she kept them to herself. At their next scheduled meeting, Natalie played the devil's advocate, thereby revealing a shrewd intellect. Also a gifted artist, Natalie came up with the idea of storyboarding their plan, to highlight any possible flaws. She also volunteered to purchase one of the essential materials proposed by Zac.

Robbie would have preferred to purchase padded underclothing for his role but that would have telegraphed their intention. Also, since a rehearsal was out of the question, the trio agreed that they would at least visit the proposed venue before fixing the date and time of execution. Once this was done, no one expressed any reservations whatsoever, as the clock slowly ticked down.

On a fairly warm afternoon, the moment was over in a flash, barely seconds, in contrast to the tense waiting period. A frame-by-frame playback would have shown Robbie slipping at the top of the staircase between the top and penultimate floors of their hometown *Maytag* store. The store architecture comprised an outhouse with a sloping roof, featuring fast-food chains and other popular eateries, adjacent to the five-floor shopping area. Conceivably, the twelve-step staircase was designed to encourage customers to stay healthy, by working off some of the calories after a meal.

In the aftermath, a small crowd had gathered around a convulsed and prone Robbie. At first, it seemed as though he was unconscious, and the angularity of his left arm suspended across the back of his neck was not reassuring. When he slowly and painfully unhooked his arm, a piercing shriek escaped his tortured windpipe. At that moment, two store security men walked up and ordered the onlookers to step back. As they contemplated the most appropriate first aid assistance to administer, Robbie moaned as he lifted his head for the first time, revealing a bleeding nose.

Genuinely shaken, Natalie hovered over Robbie and was quick to offer him her handkerchief. Meanwhile, largely unnoticed in the background, there was Zac with his phone camera recording the incident from multiple angles. The extent of Robbie's injuries could not yet be ascertained but his obvious discomfort was rather unsettling. Thankfully, he could rise and stand up; however, his dangling left arm and drooping shoulder looked suspect. Less than three minutes after the accident, a young lady who introduced herself as *Maytag*'s paramedic was on the scene. Taking charge, she held onto Robbie's right arm and gently guided him to the lowest rung of the staircase from where he had just tumbled.

"How are you feeling? Do you know where you are?" she asked, as she ran a light beam across his eyes.

"I am his partner. We had just finished eating and were on our way down when he slipped and fell...," started Natalie, before the paramedic cut her off.

"That's all right... We'll get to that later. An ambulance should be here shortly to convey your friend to the hospital," said the lady.

To staunch Robbie's nosebleed, which was yet to abate, she inserted a nasal packing into his nose in a deflated state, then slowly inflated it with a syringe. Moving expertly, gingerly she manoeuvred his crippled arm into a make-shift sling. By then, the security men had dispersed the gawkers while cordoning off the accident scene. Their objective was to return everything to normalcy and limit the fallout as best as they could. Gesturing after taking a phone call, the lady announced,

"Please secure the exit... The ambulance is less than a minute away."

Satisfied with his camera handiwork, Zac ran up and discreetly retrieved Robbie's leather tote bag, which he must have dropped when he fell at the top of the staircase, but otherwise kept his distance from his two companions. Looking down, he watched as Robbie, Natalie, and the paramedic moved towards the exit doors. When Robbie stood up and pulled back his head, he appeared to stiffen momentarily. So far, the plan had gone off better than expected. From a neutral's point of view, old Robbie looked genuinely bruised and battered, and everyone, including the security men, looked amply empathetic. He could not tell if Robbie was play-acting because his injuries were real but, if he was embellishing his performance, surely he deserved a mini *Oscar* or *BAFTA* award.

As he strode through the parking lot, he sent Natalie a *WhatsApp* message, essentially asking her to keep him posted of events via the same platform, and to avoid making voice calls for the moment. Natalie had enacted her cameo role as Robbie's distraught girlfriend as well as Zac had expected, to deflect attention away from two guys who might have thrown off a pungent scent of scepticism. Reflecting on how the day had unfolded, Zac conceded that Robbie had absolutely taken the greatest risk. But then, if he was ever going to become a great stuntman, he needed as much practice as he could get!

Although there was no practical way to conduct a dry run, Robbie had told them that it was crucial that he protected his head with his arms, to tuck his chin into his chest, ball up and roll as he fell. Of course, it was easier said than done, and better the other bloke than him, thought Zac. Unlucky that Robbie landed on his face, but hopefully he managed to protect his skull.

On Natalie's part, she had monitored the traffic around the stairs to determine the opportune time to make their move. Prior to that, Zac had detached himself from them and walked down to the lower floor, ready to capture the improvised scene. The original idea called for Natalie to spill some olive oil to facilitate Robbie's fall. However, since none of the eateries served olive oil, they switched to milkshake which was on the menu. The choreography of dropping her purse, bending down, and synchronising the spillage with Robbie's slide-and-crash was nerve-racking, but apparently she pulled it off.

On the surface, it seemed Zac's contribution was the least significant. But he knew better than that. The shoe-switch was all his idea but, more importantly, his knowledge of the British legal system and how to navigate its bureaucratic procedures could prove more crucial than what transpired beforehand.

To the uninitiated, the UK Personal Injury Claims (PIC) market is a sub-sector within the legal framework with annual turnover worth hundreds of millions of pounds. As expected, there exist hundreds of firms of solicitors who offer legal advice, and liaison with insurance companies – for a percentage of the compensation award. Many advertise a 'no win-no fee' agreement, but could be expected to retain in the range of twenty-five percent, if successful.

Zac's research had shown that there were advantages in using a solicitor. On the other hand, he was not comfortable sharing the claim proceeds with a fourth party. To be frank, the process seemed straightforward enough and he fancied himself a good negotiator, drawing from his deal-making experience with suppliers and business partners.

Interrupting Zac's daydream was the latest message from Natalie, who had gained entry into the Accident and Emergency (A & E) unit at the hospital, as Robbie's 'partner'. The hospital had confirmed the fracture of the radius bone in Robbie's left forearm, which had already been immobilised in a cast. It was estimated that it would take six to eight weeks to heal.

Poor Robbie had also been diagnosed with nasal fracture, caused by a crack in the cartilage around the bridge of his nose. He also hurt his back and indications were that he would require rest and some physiotherapy. The doctor had ordered a facial X-ray, once the swelling around Robbie's nose had subsided. Besides these injuries, he also incurred minor bruises and abrasions, which the nurses had already treated. But, significantly, Robbie was being retained overnight and kept under observation.

To the credit of *Maytag*'s store management, an official was assigned to Robbie's case on a full-time basis. When the X-ray results revealed that Robbie would require surgery, known as *rhinoplasty*, after about ten days to realign his nose, *Maytag* suggested a private procedure, if necessary. By the third day, Robbie was discharged from hospital and driven home. From the hospital bed to the ambulance, and on arrival at home, Robbie was conveyed in a wheelchair, further authenticating the injury claim.

Was it possible that Robbie's sprained back was in worse shape than he imagined, thought Zac. Waiting to receive the returning 'hero' were Zac, Natalie, and a couple of their close friends and neighbours. Zac had ordered buckets of KFC chicken and fries, as well as two Big Macs, Robbie's favourites. After the medics and *Maytag*'s representative had left, including the other guests, the two guys began the ribbing and wisecracks in earnest, while Natalie remained largely deadpan. As she helped to tidy up, the best line of the evening was delivered by Zac, mimicking an American accent,

"Robbie left home as a suave Hollywood leading man but returned to us as pug-nosed Rocky Balboa… Life just ain't fair."

CHAPTER 7

Three weeks after the accident, a designated *Maytag* official made an appointment to see Robbie in the apartment. True to their word, *Maytag* had fast-tracked the nasal operation at a private clinic and, following a successful outcome, Robbie was back at home recuperating.

When buttoned-down Mr. Zellick (who never offered his first name) showed up, he was accompanied by another man who introduced himself as Tom (breezily dispensing with his last name). Like an incongruous tag team, Tom was there as a representative of *Maytag*'s insurance company. As agreed, Zac stayed back to lend his support to Robbie.

After narrating the store accident and its aftermath in very precise prose, Mr. Zellick formally introduced his colleague who, after clearing his throat, opened his briefcase to reveal stashes of documents. Began Tom,

"First, let me say that we are sorry to be meeting under these circumstances. The management of Maytag regrets the unfortunate

accident at the store and send their best wishes for your quick recovery.

We have received and reviewed the medical reports from both hospitals, and would wish to conclude this matter as soon as possible. To proceed, there are several forms that you will need to complete... personal details such as your job history, bank details, and so on. Thereafter, our team of assessors will make a recommendation to Maytag regarding the appropriate level of compensation. Do you perhaps have any questions at this point?"

"It's pretty clear so far... please go on," replied Robbie.

"From experience, once Maytag's management signs off on the recommendation and all parties reach a settlement, the whole process could be wrapped up within a few weeks."

"Tom, if you don't mind me asking... can Robbie make a final decision on his own or does he require outside advice?" chimed in Zac.

"It's entirely up to Robbie to seek legal counsel, or not. It's his prerogative, although I imagine it would not be free. I can assure you that

we follow standard protocols in our assessment. But, like I said, you should do what you believe is in your best interest," added Tom.

It was apparent that Mr. Zellick had other appointments and, from his tone, he sounded as though he believed the meeting should be rounding up,

"Thank you very much for your time. If it's okay, I shall return by, say, 4:00 p.m. tomorrow to retrieve the completed form unless, of course, you can scan and e-mail them to me."

"No, I'd rather you come over to pick them up. Thank you both for coming over... Bye, and see you tomorrow," responded Robbie.

Prior to this meeting, Zac and Robbie had concluded that it was best to review *Maytag*'s formal settlement proposal before weighing their next move. When they eventually received an offer, the three partners had designated Zac as the intermediary who would seek to negotiate the best deal possible. If that failed, they could then pursue the option of taking legal action, by submitting a claim at the civil court. Engaging the services of a solicitor would reduce the overall 40:40:20 three-way split, with Natalie agreeing to the minority stake. When they arrived at that juncture, they would meet to agree a final strategy. Meanwhile, all they could do was wait.

Contrary to Zac's expectations, Mr. Zellick hand-delivered the offer letter two weeks after their first meeting. Addressed to Robbie, the letter captioned *'Part 36 Offer'* summarised the accident details and costs incurred, and concluded by making a final compensation award of £3,750.00 to Robbie Grant, without prejudice. Robbie had twenty-one days within which to accept or decline the offer, with no avenue for direct negotiations.

For clarification, Zac asked Mr. Zellick,

"Please can you explain what you mean by 'without prejudice'?"

"Ah, it's a legal term that says that the content of this document cannot be used as evidence in a court case; also, that this offer in no way implies an admission of open-ended liability by Maytag.

After consultations between us and our insurance company, and taking all factors into consideration, this is what we describe as a good faith offer to compensate Mr. Grant for the unfortunate accident. Of course, you are at liberty to seek legal advice before responding to the letter," answered Mr. Zellick.

Robbie felt that he had heard enough and could not wait for Mr. Zellick to depart, and virtually shut down the meeting by saying,

"Thank you very much, Mr. Zellick, for coming over and for all your support. We'll review your offer and get back shortly."

Once Mr. Zellick had left, Zac literally exploded,

"£3,750! They must be having me on. With all your injuries, surely they can't be serious…"

"But remember that they paid all my medical expenses and…," started Robbie.

"I know all that, but what about your back? How long do you think before you can return to work? They've got to do much better than that," shouted Zac.

"Anyway, when is Natalie coming over?"

"I've sent her a WhatsApp… she should be here within an hour."

When Natalie arrived, she was briefed on *Maytag*'s offer, and then Zac continued from where he stopped earlier,

"Guys, guys, let me break it down for you. First, I believe that what they've offered Robbie is ridiculous. If we had used a solicitor, it's possible that the offer could have been higher. But then, the solicitors will insist on their cut.

Moving forward, we have two options. Either we go it alone and submit Robbie's claim directly to the county court, or we engage a firm of solicitors. Some solicitors sell a no win-no fee proposition..."

Cutting in, Natalie said,

"But that shouldn't apply here since Robbie already has an offer in hand."

"You're absolutely right, Natalie. But assuming we reject the offer, apart from what we agree to pay the solicitors, usually a percentage of the final award by the court, we must also cough up about £300 as the application fee to kick off the process."

"So, which option have we agreed, assuming we reject Maytag's offer?" asked Robbie.

Sitting down for the first time since the meeting started, Zac pressed home his point,

"My recommendation is that we reject the offer. From what I discovered online, I believe we should pitch our claim at £15,000. If you disagree with me, and insist that we use solicitors, then we should increase the figure to at least £20,000 to cover their costs. The reason why I think we have a very strong case is because, the two fractures aside, the treatment on Robbie's back might take much longer. The implication is that he will need intense physiotherapy and might not be able to return to work for quite a while. I also read that he can invoke emotional distress as part of his claim. So, what do you guys think?"

At that moment, Robbie winced. It was unclear whether it was because of back pain or due to the matter-of-fact manner Zac seemed to have lost himself into what was, after all, a dubious scheme. He glanced over at Natalie, whose expression had not wavered.

To fill in the silence, Zac continued,

"To help us decide, I have drawn up a checklist of what we'll require to submit a claim. Looking through, honestly I'm not sure what value the solicitors are really adding. Besides, they might delve too deeply into the accident and begin to ask awkward questions.

So, let me tick off the list one by one... One: date of the accident. Two: time of the accident. Three: the location of the accident. Four: how the accident happened. Five: the contact details of any witnesses to the accident – that will be Natalie and me. Six: a medical report detailing the claimant's injuries, medical diagnosis, and past and future treatments. Seven: photographic evidence, if any. Eight: proof of any loss of earnings. Nine: evidence of other expenses incurred as a result of the trauma caused by the accident.

I have already downloaded the claim form from the Internet. It's called the Part 8 Claim form. Once it's completed in triplicates, we are expected to attach a cheque of about £300... I can get the exact figure later, and either hand-deliver or mail it to the Brighton County Court located near Edward Street. My suggestion is that we split the application fee three ways, okay?"

The other two partners nodded, and deep down were quite impressed with Zac's thoroughness. Apprehensive about lawyers questioning and prying into what went down, Robbie shared Zac's concern and was inching towards going it alone.

"*Hmm... I was just wondering... How do you think Maytag would react if we turn them down?*" chipped in Natalie.

"*My understanding is that, as the defendants, they will have an opportunity to respond to our legal action. They can choose to improve their offer and negotiate with Robbie. On the other hand, the case can go ahead, with a district judge assigned to the hearing. Frankly, aside from shelling out £300, I suspect we are looking at an upside here,*" said Zac, who in reality was less confident than he sounded.

"*I say, let's go for it,*" declared Robbie.

"*All in, I'm with you guys... let's do it,*" added Natalie.

CHAPTER 8

The umbrella body of *Her Majesty's Courts and Tribunals Service (HMCTS)*, under the Ministry of Justice, is responsible for the administration of justice in England and Wales. Following innumerable reforms, the *HMCTS* was established to run the judicial system - comprising criminal and civil courts - that ensures that *"the rule of law is upheld and provides access to justice for all."*

Whereas the state prosecutes an individual in a criminal case, civil court cases enable individuals or businesses to seek remedy when they believe their rights have been infringed. In the UK, county courts deal with civil, or non-criminal, matters. Contrary to expectations, the jurisdiction of most county courts covers more than a single county, with most cases being decided by a district or circuit judge sitting alone.

Although he had never fallen foul of the law, Zac had done his homework. He tried to decipher the structure of the English legal system, especially as it pertained to civil law. Less than a week after Mr. Zellick's last visit, Zac had prodded Robbie to sign and reject *Maytag*'s offer letter. Inside the comment box, he had penned his decision to pursue legal action against *Maytag*, without any further elaboration. A day before the letter was delivered by Zac, Natalie contacted the boys and suggested that perhaps they should first approach *Maytag* for an improved offer before starting any legal proceedings.

Not surprisingly, Zac rejected the idea out of hand. His contention was that the best they could expect from *Maytag* was a marginal increase, if any. Said Zac,

"The insurance companies are extremely stingy... I'm convinced that the court will be much more sympathetic when we lay out our claim in black and white. Instead of dilly-dallying, I say that we move quickly to avoid second-guessing each other."

Based on Zac's advice, the trio spent that evening filling out the downloaded application form. By identifying Robert Grant as the claimant and *Maytag Limited* as the defendant, and adding their respective contact details, *Grant v Maytag* had taken on a life of its own. However, the section of the so-called *N208 Form* which took most of their time was *Details of Claim*. Whilst the information required was mostly available in the letter received from *Maytag*, they were careful not to simply cut-and-paste. The official medical report was included, and the supplementary narrative highlighted Robbie's lingering back pain, his facial 'disfigurement', and the emotional distress that he was experiencing. As the two key witnesses, Zac and Natalie came up with two different but synchronised versions of their recollections. Last but not the least, they selected photographs from Zac's collection that best showcased and supported Robbie's claim.

For a court house, the Brighton County Court is not a particularly imposing building. It is located on William Street, just around the corner from Edward Street and the popular Victoria Gardens. From its exterior, it is a modern low-strung, brick-and-glass structure. It is the type of building that most people drive past without noticing, until the need arises for them to use its service. Robbie and his partners belonged in this category of Brightonians, until Zac drove up midday midweek, just as spring was giving way to early summer, to deposit Robbie's claim form with a cheque tucked inside the manila envelope. They had rolled the dice for the biggest stake of their young lives and, to appropriate one of those anonymous quotes, *"whatever is meant to happen always does."*

The reason why county courts encourage applicants to submit their claim forms in triplicates is quite simple. Once the application has been formally set up and given a case or claim number, and listed for a hearing, the court keeps one copy of the claim form while one sealed copy is sent to the claimant and another to the defendant, or to their solicitors if they have any. When *Maytag* received a notice of Robbie's claim, it triggered a series of activities that promptly drew in their insurers.

Like in most large retail organisations, certain funds are set aside in their annual budgets against unanticipated expenditures. This could be viewed as part of the cost of doing business on a global scale, where the odd slippages, accidents, and similar incidents on their premises are presumed. However, in the event that a company is challenged in court, this activates processes that aim to limit its corporate exposure and liability. The ad-hoc team assembled by *Maytag* included Mr. Zellick, Tom, Susan Miles representing *Maytag*'s solicitors, and a forensic private investigator, Neil Simon. The professional expertise of the two additions signified how seriously large companies respond to external threats. Simply put, they do not like to lose, since signs of perceived weakness could erode their brand equity over time.

Susan Miles worked out of the London office of Giles & Ickes LLP, the firm of solicitors retained by *Maytag* for civil cases. Although *Maytag* had opened five other outlets across the UK in less than two years, the company was headquartered in London. Ordinarily, a civil case is heard at the local court where the defendant is located. However, the one exception is when the defendant is a corporate body, in which case the jurisdiction reverts to the county court closest to the claimant. Therefore, *Grant v Maytag* was assigned to Brighton County Court, which clearly suited Robbie and his partners.

Possibly the most important member of the team was Neil Simon, a former police detective who retired at the relatively young age to set up his own private investigation practice. Long gone is the image of professionals in the field who worked out of darkened offices and wore trench coats. Neil was one of the most capable technology and cybersecurity experts in his division, and this ability gave him the impetus and confidence to set up a firm that targeted private companies. With a perpetual half-cocked smile, Neil had a disarming way about him but a razor-sharp mind that could be lethal to anyone who underestimated him. Ideologically, he was a right-of-centre voter who believed in the capitalist system, and saw it as one of his duties to protect the English way of life which he truly admired.

Professionally, Neil's firm had grown from a two-man operation to nine full-term and six part-time associates in less than three years. As he saw it, if they delivered tangible results and met their clients' expectations, his firm could expect to survive in a highly competitive but poorly regulated industry. In addition to computer forensics, which covered data recovery and security of computer networks against hacking, Neil's firm also specialised in forensic accounting, surveillance, witness location and interviewing, and insurance claims investigation. When Neil received the summons from *Maytag* to work on *Grant v Maytag*, he was determined to use the opportunity to bolster his firm's reputation.

At Brighton County Court, the court file created for *Grant v Maytag* was referred to District Judge Rick Zeppelin. For someone with such a cool name, DJ Zeppelin was, in fact, an amiable, unobtrusive jurist who just got on with the job. He was a local lad who grew up supporting Brighton & Hove Albion football club, and literally married the girl next door, Alice. With his background as a solicitor, he was elevated to the bench after acquiring technical expertise in bankruptcy and insolvency matters. However, his portfolio of duties extended to wills and trust, personal injury claims, property possession, defamation, and similar civil cases.

After studying the *Grant v Maytag* file very carefully, he sent it down to court administration for listing. The process of listing involved fixing a hearing date for the case and sending notices and sealed copies of the claim forms to both the claimant and the defendant. Within a set deadline, the defendant would be obliged to send a written defence, witness statements, and an *acknowledgment of service* back to the court. As allowed by the system, the two parties could also use this period to settle the case out of court.

Back at Maytag, the four-person team met to review the court documents, with renewed emphasis on the witness statements submitted by Zac and Natalie. There and then, the unanimous recommendation to management was to decline the option of an out-of-court settlement. Immediately, Susan Miles started preparing *Maytag*'s response, which included witness statements provided by the store's security officers at the scene and the paramedic, amongst other necessary documentation. In parallel, Neil would begin the process of interviewing and gathering independent evidence in support of a possible counterclaim.

When Robbie and his mates received the hearing date from the county court, Zac tried to ease the rising tension by saying,

"Guys, it's going to be okay, I can feel it… the good news is that Robbie's arm will still be in a cast when we attend the hearing. That should get him some sympathy form the judge…"

Robbie smiled nervously but nodded in agreement. Natalie wore her normally inscrutable look and said nothing.

Two days before the case was heard, the *Maytag* team met for a final strategy session. Neil had not come up with any suitable evidence that could support a counterclaim. Therefore, it was agreed that their solicitor's defence argument will centre on the speed of response, provision of medical assistance, and a fair market offer of final compensation.

Unlike criminal cases, civil cases are usually heard by a district or circuit judge in a closed session or court room, and the final ruling delivered by that judge after all the evidence and witness statements have been examined. Again, unlike criminal trials - which are typically characterised by jury selection, cross-examination of witnesses, opening and closing statements by the prosecution and defence lawyers, and present significant scope for courtroom drama - civil cases are relatively more subdued.

On closer examination, the latter characterisation may be true for civil matters involving damages, possession, and money claims. On the other hand, family, adoption, and divorce cases, which are also handled by county courts, are often messy affairs, and high on the emotional *Richter* scale.

The *Grant v Maytag* hearing was held in a large meeting room at Brighton County Court, rather than in open court. Robbie showed up in a smart casual outfit with his arm cast and a suitably pained expression, representing himself. In tow were Zac and Natalie, the former wearing a blue blazer without a tie while she wore a simple frock, both appearing as witnesses for the claimant. Before the court appearance, the three partners had rehearsed their lines as best as possible, and urged one another to relax and remain calm during the proceedings. Slightly uncomfortable, Robbie felt the need to ease a persistent itch underneath his cast, while Zac's palms grew sweaty when DJ Zeppelin entered the meeting room. Only Natalie seemed unaffected by the court surroundings.

Across the table facing them were Susan Miles, Mr. Zellick, one of the security guards at the scene of the accident, and the paramedic. As lawyers tend to project in a courthouse, Susan had an intimidating presence about her, partly due to her power suit, but also because the opposing side had no legal representation. But this was not a criminal case, which meant that the full authority of the hearing and the format to be followed rested with the judge.

In the event, the hearing lasted less than forty minutes. DJ Zeppelin asked a few questions to clarify what had already been documented. As agreed at their last strategy meeting, when responding to the judge's questions, Susan made no effort to dispute the facts of the case. Instead, she sounded conciliatory, by pitching *Maytag* as a good corporate citizen that had acted in good faith. Turning his attention to Robbie, the judge asked him about his recovery and rehabilitation programme. None of the witnesses was questioned or interrogated, which probably implied that the judge was satisfied with the written accounts. As a consequence, the most relieved person in that room was undoubtedly Zac.

DJ Zeppelin took notes as the hearing progressed, and could not help but reflect on how many of such cases he had adjudicated since the beginning of that year alone. Although he believed in adhering to the spirit of the law and was certainly no liberal, by instinct he tended to favour the underdog in matters involving multinationals and big companies. He saw no contradiction in his strong support for the market economic system and what he would describe as social justice. He left the meeting room for his office but returned within thirty minutes to read out his judgment.

After DJ Zeppelin had sat down and adjusted his reading glasses, he spoke in his customary measured tone,

"After considering all the facts and evidence presented by both parties in the case of Grant versus Maytag, it is ordered that:

1. *The Defendant will pay the Claimant the sum of £12,750.00, in addition to the medical expenditures already incurred by the Defendant.*
2. *The Defendant will pay the Claimant the sum of £308.00, representing the cost of this application.*
3. *All sums payable by the Claimant shall be made by the Defendant within 21 days from the date of this Order.*
4. *Either party may apply within 10 days of service to vary any of its terms.*

That concludes this hearing.

Thank you."

And that was it.

It was all over, or so they thought.

CHAPTER 9

Robbie and Zac saved the high-fives until they were safely ensconced in their apartment, away from prying eyes. Natalie smiled but remained as reserved as ever.

"I can't believe that we pulled it off...," shrieked Zac.

"Yeah, sure... I'm just glad it's over. Whenever the judge glanced in my direction, it felt like he was trying to read my mind... Phew!" exclaimed Robbie.

"What do you think, Natalie? The solicitor didn't look too pleased..." stuttered Zac.

"I say let's wait and see. Generally, companies don't like to lose, or maybe I should say lawyers," intoned Natalie.

At the other camp, the main concern was not about the quantum of the money claim, but the perception it could create if *Maytag* failed to put up a challenge. After the hearing, Mr. Zellick took to referring to the district judge as 'Led', as in *Led*

Zeppelin. Even staid Susan seemed to approve the nickname, possibly as an outlet for her professional frustration. She felt that the ruling by the judge was out of proportion but, unless some new evidence was soon unearthed, her handling of the case might be called into question by the client and her firm. On track to become a partner within three years, she needed to pull out all the stops for clients like *Maytag*, in order to achieve her dream. Although she could barely tolerate the private investigator, Neil Simon, with his condescending manner, it dawned on her that he might hold the key to this case, if there was any unexplored angle.

Neil had never hidden his disdain for corporate types, and it could be said that he enjoyed getting under their skin. Confident in his own abilities and a rebel by nature, his attitude was that he thought differently from people he dismissively described as unimaginative. Based on his exposure to information technology and cybersecurity, he was conscious of just how naïve and vulnerable most lay people were about the digital world. Furthermore, although *millennials* might perceive him to be old enough to be their dad or uncle, Neil was in fact extremely savvy about how the media, especially social media, was influencing the new generation.

After reviewing all the materials and documents provided by *Maytag*, the insurance company and the solicitors, Neil narrowed his investigation to the security video tapes and the claimant's two key witnesses. His investigation had already established the close relationship between the claimant and the two witnesses, which explained why they went shopping together. Forensic examination of the accident scene was impossible due to the elapsed time.

As a result, he had nothing to rely upon except oral feedback, photographic evidence, as well as CCTV images. Prior to the store accident, he noticed that Robbie left the table he was sharing with his friends. Nothing unusual about that, except that he carried his carry-all bag with him. On second thought, that would be normal for a lady who wanted to touch up her makeup, but a guy? Robbie returned to his mates about seven minutes later, according to the video time-stamp.

The other disturbing observation was that the claimant's male colleague, Zac whom he dubbed *Curly* by virtue of his mop-head, left the other two behind at their table and descended to the lower floor before the accident occurred. *Curly* then proceeded to capture such an unusual number of photographs that would have made a photojournalist proud. As Neil watched and re-watched *Curly* prance around with his camera glued to his face, a flash bulb suddenly went off in his head.

Distinct from older generations who existed mostly in an analogue world, younger people are perpetually online – consuming and sharing information on popular sites like *Facebook*, *YouTube* and *Instagram*. This was a generation that would be baffled if its online habits were described as exhibitionist by dowdier old-fashioned adults. Neil decided that maybe he should turn his attention to the social media activities of the three characters now in his crosshairs. With his range of surreptitious skill sets, Neil knew that he would not require a formal court warrant to access their online accounts.

Within seventy-two hours, Neil concluded that he had made a breakthrough in his investigation and so he contacted *Maytag* to set up a review meeting.

At the meeting, Neil wasted no time in presenting the new evidence that he believed would aid *Maytag*'s counterclaim, and hopefully overturn DJ Zeppelin's judgment. Neil took several questions from Susan that probed his hypothesis, sounding very much like a cross-examination. Without adjusting his smirk for a second, Neil appeared to enjoy the grilling session. At the end, Neil's technical expertise and forensic evidence seemed to have convinced the entire team that they were on solid ground.

Before the meeting was adjourned, an agreement was reached that the solicitors should immediately apply to the county court to set aside the judgment against *Maytag*.

Susan realised that they had three options, going forward. The next phase could be conducted without a court hearing, by telephone hearing, or with a hearing. To save time and money, either of the first two options would be ideal but, with the type of visual evidence that Neil would have to present, there was no way they could avoid asking for a listing date. She got one of her junior associates to fill out the *N244 Application Notice* form. Entered under the section asking what order they would like the court to review, it stated: '*This is an application to set aside the judgment delivered by District Judge Rick Zeppelin, based on fresh evidence to be presented at the next hearing.*' After the Brighton County Court received this application, along with a £255 fee, the new hearing date was listed and then communicated to all the parties by mail.

When Robbie's mail arrived, it would not be an exaggeration to state that his heart missed a beat. Scorched, he felt like throwing up all over the court document. As if stung by a wasp, Zac let fly a string of colourful expletives, and then moaned out loud,

"*Robbie, what do you think is going on here? I thought we were home and dry...*"

"*I honestly have no clue. For them to make such a request implies that they have a new piece of evidence... but what could that be?*"

"*For the life of me, I can't think of anything yet... But whatever happens, we cannot allow you to attend the hearing alone. Natalie and I will accompany you, okay?*"

"*Sure... Thanks, Zac. That makes me feel better already. Not...*"

Totally unfazed and sounding almost cocky, Neil began his slide presentation by projecting from his laptop onto a screen located directly opposite DJ Zeppelin.

Coolly, he opened by calling out the claimant and his two accomplices as scammers, who attempted to defraud his client. Even though he had no concrete proof, he surmised that Robbie had gone into the men's room to swap his shoes just before the accident occurred. In the CCTV video, which he had spliced with his presentation, he showed Robbie walking very slowly back to his seat, while seeming to hug the corridor wall. After Zac had left the table, the video then showed Natalie holding up Robbie's elbow as they moved towards the stairs. Unfortunately, the frames leading up to the fall were obscured because several customers were trailing behind Robbie and Natalie.

Ever so dramatic, Neil paused before he began to display a series of still photographs that he claimed were taken by Zac. The clincher was an image snapped at an acute angle that showed Robbie with his face down, but with the soles of his shoes turned up. Neil then went on show magnified images of the shoe soles – the first was times 2, the next times 10, and finally times 25 magnification.

According to Neil, there in full glare was the forensic proof that Robbie's shoes had been intentionally 'sandpapered' or filed with an abrasive tool. At the highest magnification, the outsole of the shoes was clearly shown to have been tampered with, presumably to reduce its grip and water resistance. For added effect, Neil then juxtaposed an image of the outsole of a similar shoe brand, unadorned, next to Robbie's. As the saying goes, everyone in the meeting room could hear a pin drop. When Neil ended his presentation, the lights were switched back on, at which point Robbie wished the ground would open up and swallow him.

DJ Zeppelin looked around the room, as he considered his next decision. After what seemed like an eternity but was no longer than ninety seconds, he asked Robbie, Zac and Natalie to follow him into his office, while calling time out. An announcement would be made as soon as the hearing was due to reconvene.

Inside the judge's office, with no note-taker present, DJ Zeppelin went straight to the point,

"Since you have no legal representation, by choice I imagine, let me make myself as clear as possible.

The three of you are this close to being held in contempt of this court," he said, holding up two fingers.

"In layman's language, that means that you have conspired to misrepresent your actions in relation to the defendant, and also you disrespected Her Majesty's Court and her officers.

Taking into consideration your age and naiveté, I shall offer you two stark choices. First, I can refer this case to a Crown Court where Maytag may seek legal redress, and you will be tried as co-defendants.

Your second choice is this: confess your misdemeanour right now, in my office, and then I might decide to use my legal prerogative to wrap up the case at this hearing.

If you wish, you can huddle outside in my waiting room and then return as soon as possible to give me your response."

Robbie and Zac looked at one another intently, but Natalie stared straight ahead without betraying any emotion. Deflated and in total resignation, Robbie simply nodded his quiet assent, almost as if they had planned for this contingency. With that cue, Zac spoke up,

"Um... thank you, sir... I mean, Your Honour. We will not wish to prolong this hearing any further or to waste any more of your time...

It all started as a prank which then developed into an idea for which I take full responsibility. Yes, Your Honour, I planned the whole thing and I am terribly sorry it has led to this moment."

Neither Robbie nor Natalie said a word. They simply hung their heads, waiting for the judge to respond.

"Hmm... I thought the evidence presented by the defendant was highly convincing. The three of you have broken the law and you've been found out. Nevertheless, you did the right thing by confessing your misdemeanour.

Okay, go back into the room to await my final ruling."

Twenty-five minutes later, the hearing resumed when DJ Zeppelin walked back into the hushed room. Briefly, for the first time since they met each other, Susan managed to crack a smile in conversation with Neil. It was evident that both of them, including Mr. Zellick, cared more about winning the case than seeking retributions. Winners tend to rise to the top in a corporate environment, whereas losers are classified as nothing but whiners.

Nevertheless, they were wary enough to recognise that the domain of personal injury fraud had continued to spread across the UK. Despite the amateurism and desperation often exhibited by many of the perpetrators, the pace of car accident and workplace injury claims seemed to be growing.

Before reading out his judgment, DJ Zeppelin began with a preamble,

"We should all be proud that we live in a nation governed by the rule of law. Our judiciary is an exemplar that is admired worldwide for its openness and robustness.

The case before us, Grant v Maytag, could have had a rather different outcome. But I am pleased that the defendant's doggedness has ensured that justice has prevailed.

In the last half hour or so, I managed to extract from the claimant and his colleagues a confession that necessarily overturns my earlier judgment. Based on the forensic evidence presented by the defendant today, their misdemeanour was

fully exposed. While a custodial sentence is off the table, rest assured that they shall pay a price for their actions.

At this juncture, I'd like to invite the defendant's solicitor to respond before I pass my final judgment."

Although she did not have a prepared statement, Susan's legal training and courtroom experience kicked in at that moment. Blithely ignoring Robbie, she stood up and said,

"Thank you, Your Honour. On behalf of Maytag and others here representing the defendant, I feel extremely gratified that our client's show of good faith throughout this case has endured.

As I said at the beginning of the proceedings, the management of Maytag took full responsibility for the medical care and rehabilitation of the claimant – unconditionally.

In concluding this case, we have full confidence in the Court's discretion to ensure that justice is seen to be done.

Thank you, Your Honour."

At that point, the court officer sitting next to the stenographer asked Robbie, Zac and Natalie to stand up. Reading from his handwritten notes, DJ Zeppelin declared,

"Based upon the new forensic evidence orally presented by the defendant, it is ordered by this Court that:

> *1. A complete and truthful narrative of the events preceding and following the accident at the Maytag Store should be documented by this Court.*
> - *That this confessional statement be duly endorsed by the Claimant and his two accomplices.*
> *2. The medical expenditure so far incurred by the Defendant shall be deemed as tax-deductible. However, the court expenses of the Defendant shall be refunded by mutual consent.*
> *3. As recompense for their misdemeanours, it is ordered that:*
> - *Mr. Zac Levin and Ms Natalie Jones shall be subject to 30 days of community service, the details of which will be communicated to them within 48 hours.*

- *In light of his continuing recuperation, Mr. Robbie Grant shall serve a similar sentence, once he has fully recovered, as certified by a medical practitioner.*

This hearing is hereby concluded."

The sentencing letters from the county court for all three were dispatched simultaneously. Robbie's stated, as follows:

"Dear Mr. Grant,

Following your full recovery from your injuries, the Court has ordered that you report to the Juvenile Rehabilitation Centre for a period of 30 days.

You will be expected to do the following:

a) Pick up litter for an hour every morning along London Road, Brighton.
b) On alternate days, clean the graffiti on along the same street.
c) Spend a minimum of two hours each day at the Juvenile Rehabilitation Centre performing chores ordered by the centre's administrator.

At the successful completion of your community service, a duly signed discharge letter shall be issued to you by a designated court officer.

Yours faithfully,

Brighton County Court."

London Road? Yes, that *London Road* with its open markets! Against all odds and with an ironic twist of fate, Robbie faced the imminent prospect of running into his folks, *Pop!*, whenever he was fit enough to begin his court-mandated community service.

Squaring his shoulders, he groped for how he could *use this difficulty* to turn around his fortunes... for starters, by steering clear of bare-knuckle and gratuitous stunts.

www.ingramcontent.com/pod-product-compliance
Lightning Source LLC
Chambersburg PA
CBHW020447220526
45464CB00002B/903